EXPLORING DINOSAURS & PREHISTORIC CREATURES

PELYCOSAURS

By Susan H. Gray

THE CHILD'S WORLD
CHANHASSEN, MINNESOTA

The Child's World®

Published in the United States of America by The Child's World®
PO Box 326, Chanhassen, MN 55317-0326
800-599-READ
www.childsworld.com

Content Adviser:
Brian Huber, PhD,
Curator, Department
of Paleobiology,
Smithsonian
National Museum
of Natural History,
Washington DC

Photo Credits: Illustration by Karen Carr: 14, 23; Stan Osolinski/Corbis: 7; Layne
Kennedy/Corbis: 12; Angela Hampton, Ecoscene/Corbis: 19; Jonathan Blair/Corbis:
25; Kevin Schafer/Corbis: 27; Mike Fredericks: 17, 20; Douglas Henderson: 21; John
Sibbick/The Natural History Museum, London: 4, 8; Michael Long/The Natural
History Museum, London: 6; Chase Studio/Photo Researchers, Inc.: 5; Scott Camazine/
Photo Researchers, Inc.: 9; Barbara Strnadova/Photo Researchers, Inc.: 10; M. Kulyk/
Photo Researchers, Inc.: 11; Sinclair Stammers/Photo Researchers, Inc.: 15; Early Triassic
paleogeographic map by C. R. Scotese, © 2004, PALEOMAP Project (www.scotese.com)/
© 2001, Atlas of Earth History, Volume 1, Paleogeography, PALEOMAP Project,
Arlington, Texas, 52 pp.: 24; Ken Lucas/Visuals Unlimited: 13; Brandon Cole/Visuals
Unlimited: 16; Albert Copley/Visuals Unlimited: 26; The Age of Reptiles, a mural by
Rudolph F. Zallinger. Copyright © 1966, 1975, 1985, 1989, Peabody Museum of
Natural History, Yale University, New Haven, CT: 18.

The Child's World®: Mary Berendes, Publishing Director

Editorial Directions, Inc.: E. Russell Primm, Editorial Director; Pam Rosenberg,
Line Editor; Katie Marsico, Associate Editor; Matthew Messbarger, Editorial Assistant;
Susan Hindman, Copy Editor; Melissa McDaniel, Proofreader; Tim Griffin/IndexServ,
Indexer; Olivia Nellums, Fact Checker; Dawn Friedman, Photo Researcher; Linda
S. Koutris, Photo Selector

Original cover art by Todd Marshall

The Design Lab: Kathleen Petelinsek, Design and Page Production

Library of Congress Cataloging-in-Publication Data
Gray, Susan Heinrichs.
  Pelycosaurs / by Susan H. Gray.
    p. cm. — (Exploring dinosaurs & prehistoric creatures)
  Includes index.
  ISBN 1-59296-411-7 (libr. bd. : alk. paper) 1. Pelycosauria—Juvenile literature.
I. Title.
  QE862.P3G75 2005
  567.9'3—dc22   2004018081

TABLE OF CONTENTS

CHAPTER ONE

A Slow Morning

It had stormed all night long, and none of the pelycosaurs (PELL-ih-kuh-SAWRZ) had gotten much sleep. Even as the sun was rising, the air was still chilly and damp. On days like this, it was hard to get moving.

The storm had been especially wild, with howling winds and loud thunderclaps. The pelycosaurs were not used to so much noise. They were never

For millions of years, pelycosaurs dominated the Earth.

bothered by thundering footsteps because dinosaurs didn't exist yet. They had never heard screeches or cries from the air because there were no birds. Once in a while, some ocean-

Dinosaurs, such as these hadrosaurs, didn't exist when pelycosaurs walked on Earth.

dwelling animal splashed at the surface. But all in all, things were pretty quiet.

Now it was morning, and the storm had passed. All was peaceful again, and the skies were clear. *Ophiacodon* (oh-fee-AK-oh-don) stretched out in the sunlight. As he warmed up,

Varanosaurus *was about 5 feet (1.5 meters) long and resembled the modern-day monitor lizard.*

he started to feel a bit livelier. A few feet away, *Varanosaurus* (vuh-RAN-oh-SAWR-uhss) lifted her heavy eyelids and closed them again. *Dimetrodon* (dy-MET-roh-don) was more alert than the others. He had been awake for more than an hour and had begun moving about. Still, this would be a long day for the drowsy pelycosaurs. If they were lucky, tonight would be quiet and they'd catch up on their sleep.

CHAPTER TWO

WHAT WERE THE PELYCOSAURS?

Pelycosaurs were animals that lived from about 290 million to 250 million years ago. They died out long before the dinosaurs appeared. The name *pelycosaur* comes from Greek words meaning "basin lizard" or "bowl lizard." This refers to the shape of the animal's hip bones.

Pelycosaurs had lizardlike bodies and tails. They were built low to the ground and walked on four

Pelycosaurs had short legs, long tails, and looked a lot like modern-day lizards, such as this collared lizard.

Earth was home to a variety of pelycosaurs during the Permian (PER-mee-uhn) period.

legs. Their legs were sprawled out to the sides, much like those of

modern-day lizards.

The creatures came in several different shapes and sizes. Some

were broad, barrel-shaped animals, while others were slender. The

smallest pelycosaurs were about 20 inches (50 centimeters) long, and

the largest were more than 11 feet (3.4 m) in length. Some had tiny, undersized heads, while others had heads that seemed much too big for their bodies. Some had sails on their backs supported by slender, bony spines, while others had sails held up by thick, knobby spines. Still others had no sails at all.

Although there were great differences among the pelycosaurs, they all had one thing in common. Each one had a single hole on the right and left side of its skull, right behind its eyes. This may not sound important, but only the pelycosaurs, their closest relatives, and **mammals**

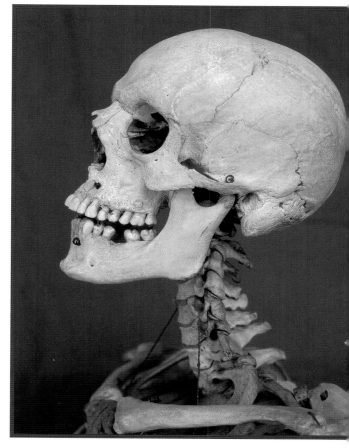

A human skull has a single hole on each side, right behind its eyes. This is a characteristic that pelycosaurs share with mammals.

(including human beings) have these single holes. In general,

reptiles have two holes on each side of their skull, or they have

no holes at all. Dinosaurs, for instance, had two holes, and turtles

have none. These holes provided spaces for muscles to pass through.

The pelycosaurs were unusual for having the single holes. While

they looked like dinosaurs and other reptiles, they didn't have the

usual reptile skulls. At the same time, they looked nothing like

mammals, yet they had mammal-like skulls.

Dinosaur skulls, such as this Velociraptor *(vuh-LAHS-ih-RAP-ter)*
skull, helped scientists determine that pelycosaurs were not dinosaurs.

HOLES IN THEIR HEADS

The holes in animals' skulls can tell us a lot about the animals themselves. They tell us how the animals stood and held their heads up, how they experienced their environment, and much more.

An animal's skull holds its brain. A bundle of nerves called the spinal cord comes out from the brain and runs down the back. Where it leaves the brain, the cord passes through a big hole at the base of the skull. In animals that stand straight up, such as humans, the hole is at the bottom of the skull. In animals that slouch, such as chimpanzees, the hole is a little farther up on the back of the skull. In four-legged animals that hold their heads straight out, such as alligators, the hole is at the very back of the skull.

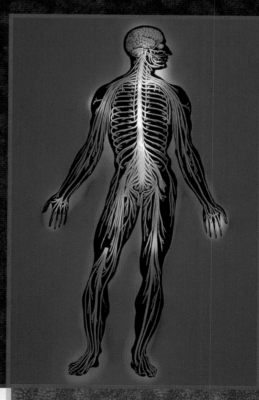

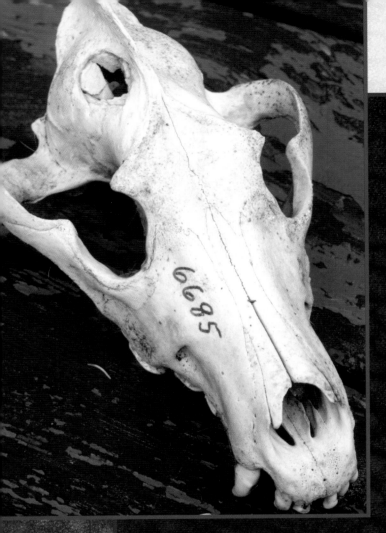

across a wide area but are unable to see in three dimensions. Such animals include birds and turtles.

Holes for the nose also tell us something. Animals that have a good sense of smell often have big nose holes and air passageways in the skull. Animals that rely less on smell and more on their other senses often have smaller nasal openings.

Suppose you found an animal skull in your backyard. The skull had one big hole at the back, two large eye holes aiming forward, and two small holes for the nose. What would these holes tell you about the animal?

Eye sockets are two other holes in the skull. These holes point forward in animals that have good depth vision, such as wolves and tigers. The holes point out to the sides in animals that see

CHAPTER THREE

HOW DID PELYCOSAURS SPEND THEIR TIME?

We can tell a lot about how the pelycosaurs lived simply by looking at their **fossil** skeletons. Pelycosaurs were built low to the ground, with short legs that went out to the sides. Because of their body structure, pelycosaurs had to walk on four legs. They could not rear up on their hind legs or jump. As they walked, they

Many Dimetrodon *fossils have been found in the United States in Texas and Oklahoma.*

Some pelycosaurs ate the plants in their environment. Others were meat eaters who ate reptiles, fish, and maybe even other pelycosaurs.

dragged their heavy tails along the ground. Some pelycosaurs may have been able to float and swim underwater like modern-day alligators.

Because of their low build, pelycosaurs had to look for food on the ground or in the water. Some pelycosaurs ate ferns and other low-lying plants, while others went after crawling insects. Meat-eating pelycosaurs probably ate reptiles, fish, and even other pelycosaurs.

Although many pelycosaurs had big, bulky bodies, this does not mean they were slow-moving animals. The meat eaters had to be quick to catch their prey.

Pelycosaurs were probably among the first animals to lay eggs on dry land. It is likely that their eggs had shells that were hard or leathery. The shells might also have had many tiny pores that allowed gases to pass through. Such shells would have kept the baby pelycosaurs safe and moist until they were ready to hatch.

Scientists have found many fossilized dinosaur eggs (above), but no pelycosaur eggs have ever been found. Still, scientists believe that pelycosaurs were one of the first animals to lay eggs on land.

No one knows how pelycosaurs cared for their young. Mothers may have laid eggs in warm sand and then abandoned them, much like modern-day sea turtles do. Or perhaps they laid eggs in the center of an earthen nest, as certain dinosaurs did. So far, no one has discovered either pelycosaur eggs or nests, so the early lives of these prehistoric creatures remain a mystery.

A loggerhead turtle lays its eggs in the sand on a beach. Pelycosaurs may have laid eggs in much the same way, but scientists don't know for sure because no pelycosaur eggs or nests have ever been found.

CHAPTER FOUR

SOME DIFFERENT PELYCOSAURS

There were several different types of pelycosaurs.

Little *Archaeothyris* (AR-kee-oh-THY-riss) is the oldest

pelycosaur known. At 20 inches (50 cm), it was also one of

the smallest. Its sharp teeth show that it was probably a

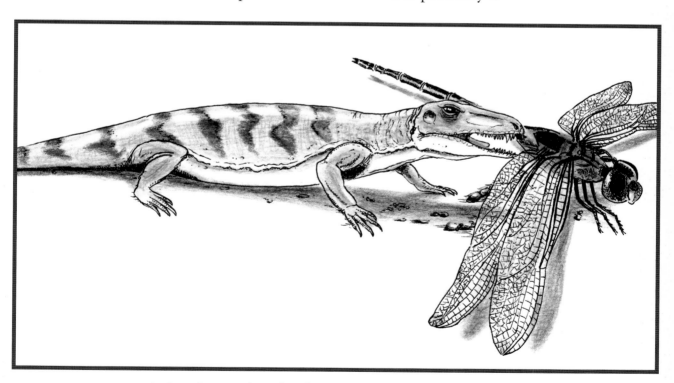

Archaeothyris is the earliest-known pelycosaur. It was about the same size as some of the large dragonflies that lived at the same time.

meat eater. *Archaeothyris* lived in warm, moist forests about

290 million years ago. Its fossils have been found only in Nova

Scotia, Canada.

At 5 to 12 feet (1.5 to 3.7 m) in length, *Ophiacodon* was much

Ophiacodon *(center) had as many as 55 teeth in each jaw.*

bigger than *Archaeothyris*. Its jaws were also filled with many sharp teeth, and some scientists believe it ate fish. Many *Ophiacodon* fossils have been found in North America.

Cotylorhynchus *had an unusual snout that has been compared to the snout of a pig (above).*

Cotylorhynchus (ko-TY-lo-RING-kuhss) was one of the largest pelycosaurs and reached a length of 13 feet (4 m). This creature had a most unusual snout. It was large and **flexible** and hung over the front of the mouth, much like the snout of a pig. The animal had a barrel-shaped body, large limbs, and a small head.

Elliotsmithia (EL-ee-uht-SMITH-ee-uh) was a small

pelycosaur that lived in what is now the country of South Africa.

Compared to some of the bulkier pelycosaurs, it was sleek and

lightly built. The teeth of *Elliotsmithia* had sharp edges on the

front and back that would have been good for cutting. The teeth

also curved backward, pointing toward the throat.

One of the most unusual-looking pelycosaurs was *Edaphosaurus*

(ee-DAFF-oh-SAWR-uhss). It was a large plant-eating animal with

Elliotsmithia *fossils have been found in South Africa.*

Edaphosaurus was a large pelycosaur that was about 11 feet (3.5 m) long and weighed about 660 pounds (299 kilograms).

little peglike teeth. Rising from its back was a large, finlike structure

supported by tall spines. The spines rose up from the backbone.

Spines closest to the head bent forward, and those nearest the tail

curved backward. Some of the spines were huge, almost like clubs.

Some spines had bumps, knobs, and crossbars along their sides.

Scientists have found *Edaphosaurus* fossils in Texas and in Europe.

DYNAMIC, DAZZLING *DIMETRODON*

Dimetrodon is one of the best-known pelycosaurs. At 11.5 feet (3.5 m), it was certainly one of the longest. At more than 400 pounds (181 kg), it was one of the heaviest. And with a mouth crammed full of sharp teeth, it was undoubtedly one of the most frightening.

But the thing that made *Dimetrodon* especially impressive was its magnificent sail. The sail was a huge flap of skin that rose from the animal's back. Long spines sticking up from the backbones supported it.

Scientists have suggested different purposes for the sail. Some say that the sail was used for thermoregulation (THER-moh-REG-yoo-LAY-shuhn). This means that *Dimetrodon* might have used the sail to control its body temperature. When *Dimetrodon*'s temperature was too low, the animal became sluggish, or lazy. To warm up, it might have stood with its sail in the sunshine. Warm rays hitting the sail would heat up the blood pulsing through it. If *Dimetrodon* got too hot, perhaps it stood in a shady, breezy spot. The blood in the sail would cool down, helping to lower the animal's temperature.

Some scientists think that the sail was used to fool enemies into thinking that *Dimetrodon* was even bigger than it was. Many modern-day animals use this trick to scare off attackers. Puffer fish blow up to twice their size whenever they feel threatened.

Maybe the sail helped *Dimetrodon* defend its territory. Modern-day male tree lizards do this by showing off a colored skin flap on their throats.

Perhaps male *Dimetrodon* used their sails to attract mates. Male animals often show off their best features to attract females. Peacocks spread their tail feathers, and frogs sing out with their best croaks. Maybe *Dimetrodon* rocked back and forth, showing off his wonderful sail. He might have arched his back, making the sail look even more majestic.

Whatever its purpose, the sail must have been very important. It doubled *Dimetrodon*'s height, making him one of the most impressive animals around.

CHAPTER FIVE

THE WORLD OF
THE PELYCOSAURS

oday, Earth is made up of several great landmasses called continents. Large oceans separate the continents. When the pelycosaurs lived, Earth was quite different.

About 280 million years ago, most of the landmasses were packed closely together into one big supercontinent. The landmass—sometimes called Pangea (pan-JEE-uh)—reached from the

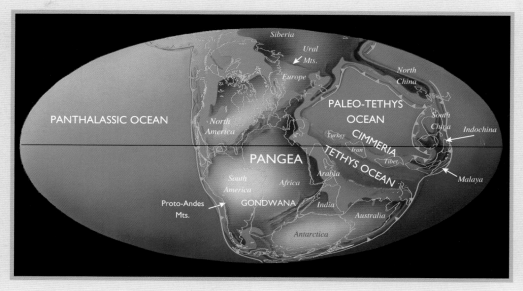

Most of Earth's landmasses formed one huge supercontinent when the pelycosaurs were alive.

North Pole to the South Pole. South America was up against Africa.

Greenland was touching Canada. Australia and Antarctica were side by

side. Pelycosaurs lived on this great supercontinent.

At that time, the northern and southern regions of the continent

were frozen solid. Large areas were completely covered in thick layers

The oceans were home to many creatures that lived at the same time as the pelycosaurs.

When pelycosaurs walked on Earth, dragonflies were very large. Fossils of dragonflies with wingspans up to 2.5 feet (76 cm) have been found in Kansas.

of ice. At the **equator,** however, it was warm and humid. Swamps and deep, lush forests were common. Huge dragonflies buzzed overhead. Millipedes the size of surfboards scuttled about the forest floor. In these warm, damp areas, pelycosaurs roamed about—some eating fish, some eating forest plants, and others feasting on the millipedes.

As time went on, Earth warmed up and the ice sheets began to melt. The air became drier, and the swamps slowly disappeared. Plants that were suited for dry conditions sprang up and began to spread. Cone-bearing trees and **ginkgos** became more common. As Earth warmed up and its plant life changed, Earth's animals changed as well. By 250 million years ago, not a single pelycosaur remained.

The leaves of the ginkgo tree are unusual. Ginkgos became common around the time of the pelycosaurs, and one kind of ginkgo tree still exists today.

Glossary

equator (i-KWAY-tur) The equator is an imaginary line around Earth that separates it into the Northern Hemisphere and Southern Hemisphere. About 280 million years ago, temperatures at the equator were warm and humid.

flexible (FLEK-suh-buhl) Something that is flexible bends easily. *Cotylorhynchus* had a flexible snout.

fossil (FOSS-uhl) A fossil is something left behind by an ancient plant or animal. Scientists can tell a lot about pelycosaurs by studying their fossil skeletons.

ginkgos (GIN-kohz) Ginkgos are small trees with fan-shaped leaves. Ginkgos and cone-bearing trees grow well in dry conditions.

mammals (MAM-uhlz) Mammals are animals that are warm-blooded, have backbones, and feed their young with milk made by the bodies of the mothers. Pelycosaurs did not look like mammals, but they had mammal-like skulls.

reptiles (REP-tilez) Reptiles are air-breathing animals that have backbones and are usually covered with scales or plates. Pelycosaurs looked like dinosaurs and other reptiles.

Did You Know?

▸ Scientists cannot agree on what kind of animals the pelycosaurs were. Some say they were reptiles. Others say they were mammals. Some call the pelycosaurs mammal-like reptiles, and others say they belong in a group of their own.

▸ *Dimetrodon* had grooves running up and down their long, bony spines. These grooves may have housed large blood vessels.

▸ More pelycosaur bones have been discovered in Oklahoma and Texas than in any other state.

How to Learn More

AT THE LIBRARY

Palmer, Douglas, and Barry Cox (editor). *The Simon & Schuster Encyclopedia of Dinosaurs & Prehistoric Creatures: A Visual Who's Who of Prehistoric Life.* New York: Simon & Schuster, 1999.

Rhodes, Frank H. T., Paul R. Shaffer, and Herbert S. Zim. *Fossils: A Golden Guide from St. Martin's Press.* New York: St. Martin's Press, 2001.

ON THE WEB

Visit our home page for lots of links about pelycosaurs:
http://www.childsworld.com/links.html
NOTE TO PARENTS, TEACHERS, AND LIBRARIANS: We routinely verify our Web links to make sure they're safe, active sites—so encourage your readers to check them out!

PLACES TO VISIT OR CONTACT

AMERICAN MUSEUM OF NATURAL HISTORY
To view numerous fossils and learn more about prehistoric creatures
Central Park West at 79th Street
New York, NY 10024-5192
212/769-5100

CARNEGIE MUSEUM OF NATURAL HISTORY
To view a variety of dinosaur skeletons, as well as fossils of other extinct animals
4400 Forbes Avenue
Pittsburgh, PA 15213
412/622-3131

SMITHSONIAN NATIONAL MUSEUM OF NATURAL HISTORY
To see several fossil exhibits and take special behind-the-scenes tours
10th Street and Constitution Avenue NW
Washington, DC 20560-0166
202/357-2700

The Geologic Time Scale

CAMBRIAN PERIOD

Date: 540 million to 505 million years ago
Most major animal groups appeared by the end of this period. Trilobites were common and algae became more diversified.

ORDOVICIAN PERIOD

Date: 505 million to 440 million years ago
Marine life became more diversified. Crinoids and blastoids appeared, as did corals and primitive fish. The first land plants appeared. The climate changed greatly during this period—it began as warm and moist, but temperatures ultimately dropped. Huge glaciers formed, causing sea levels to fall.

SILURIAN PERIOD

Date: 440 million to 410 million years ago
Glaciers melted, sea levels rose, and Earth's climate became more stable. Plants with vascular systems developed. This means they had parts that helped them to conduct food and water.

DEVONIAN PERIOD

Date: 410 million to 360 million years ago
Fish became more diverse, as did land plants. The first trees and forests appeared at this time, and the earliest seed-bearing plants began to grow. The first land-living vertebrates and insects appeared. Fossils also reveal evidence of the first ammonoids and amphibians. The climate was warm and mild.

CARBONIFEROUS PERIOD

Date: 360 million to 286 million years ago
The climate was warm and humid, but cooled toward the end of the period. Coal swamps dotted the landscape, as did a multitude of ferns. The earliest reptiles existed on Earth. Pelycosaurs such as *Edaphosaurus* evolved toward the end of the Carboniferous period.

PERMIAN PERIOD

Date: 286 million to 248 million years ago
Algae, sponges, and corals were common on the ocean floor. Amphibians and reptiles were also prevalent at this time, as were seed-bearing plants and conifers. This period ended with the largest mass extinction on Earth. This may have been caused by volcanic activity or the formation of glaciers and the lowering of sea levels.

TRIASSIC PERIOD

Date: 248 million to 208 million years ago
The climate during this period was warm and dry. The first true mammals appeared, as did frogs, salamanders, and lizards. Evergreen trees made up much of the plant life. The first dinosaurs, including *Coelophysis*, existed on Earth. In the skies, pterosaurs became the earliest winged reptiles to take flight. In the seas, ichthyosaurs and plesiosaurs made their appearance.

JURASSIC PERIOD

Date: 208 million to 144 million years ago
The climate of the Jurassic period was warm and moist. The first birds appeared at this time, and plant life was more diverse and widespread. Although dinosaurs didn't even exist in the beginning of the Triassic period, they ruled Earth by Jurassic times. *Allosaurus, Apatosaurus, Archaeopteryx, Brachiosaurus, Compsognathus, Diplodocus, Ichthyosaurus, Plesiosaurus,* and *Stegosaurus* were just a few of the prehistoric creatures that lived during this period.

CRETACEOUS PERIOD

Date: 144 million to 65 million years ago
The climate of the Cretaceous period was fairly mild. Many modern plants developed, including those with flowers. With flowering plants came a greater diversity of insect life. Birds further developed into two types: flying and flightless. Prehistoric creatures such as *Ankylosaurus, Edmontosaurus, Iguanodon, Maiasaura, Oviraptor, Psittacosaurus, Spinosaurus, Triceratops, Troodon, Tyrannosaurus rex,* and *Velociraptor* all existed during this period. At the end of the Cretaceous period came a great mass extinction that wiped out the dinosaurs, along with many other groups of animals.

TERTIARY PERIOD

Date: 65 million to 1.8 million years ago
Mammals were extremely diversified at this time, and modern-day creatures such as horses, dogs, cats, bears, and whales developed.

QUATERNARY PERIOD

Date: 1.8 million years ago to today
Temperatures continued to drop during this period. Several periods of glacial development led to what is known as the Ice Age. Prehistoric creatures such as glyptodonts, mammoths, mastodons, *Megatherium,* and saber-toothed cats roamed Earth. A mass extinction of these animals occurred approximately 10,000 years ago. The first human beings evolved during the Quaternary period.

Index

About the Author

Susan H. Gray has bachelor's and master's degrees in zoology and has taught college-level courses in biology. She first fell in love with fossil hunting while studying paleontology in college. In her 25 years as an author, she has written many articles for scientists and researchers, and many science books for children. Susan enjoys gardening, traveling, and playing the piano. She and her husband, Michael, live in Cabot, Arkansas.